Mr. & Mrs.

_____

_____

Anniversary Guest List
Names and Thoughts

Anniversary Guest List

Name :

Message or Thoughts:

_____

_____

Name

Message or Thoughts:

_____

_____

Name :

Message or Thoughts:

_____

_____

Name

Message or Thoughts:

_____

_____

Name :

Message or Thoughts:

_____

_____

Anniversary Guest List

Name : _____

Message or Thoughts: _____

_____

_____

Name _____

Message or Thoughts: _____

_____

_____

Name : _____

Message or Thoughts: _____

_____

_____

Name _____

Message or Thoughts: _____

_____

_____

Name : _____

Message or Thoughts: _____

_____

_____

Anniversary Guest List

Name :

Message or Thoughts:

_____

_____

Name

Message or Thoughts:

_____

_____

Name :

Message or Thoughts:

_____

_____

Name

Message or Thoughts:

_____

_____

Name :

Message or Thoughts:

_____

_____

Anniversary Guest List

Name :

Message or Thoughts:

_____

_____

Name

Message or Thoughts:

_____

_____

Name :

Message or Thoughts:

_____

_____

Name

Message or Thoughts:

_____

_____

Name :

Message or Thoughts:

_____

_____

Anniversary Guest List

Name :

Message or Thoughts:

_____

_____

_____

_____

Name

Message or Thoughts:

_____

_____

_____

_____

Name :

Message or Thoughts:

_____

_____

_____

_____

Name

Message or Thoughts:

_____

_____

_____

_____

Name :

Message or Thoughts:

_____

_____

_____

_____

Anniversary Guest List

Name : 🌿 _____
_____

Message or Thoughts: ✉️
_____
_____
_____

Name 🌷 _____
_____

Message or Thoughts: 🕊️
_____
_____
_____

Name : 🌿 _____
_____

Message or Thoughts: ✉️
_____
_____
_____

Name 🌷 _____
_____

Message or Thoughts: 🕊️
_____
_____
_____

Name : 🌿 _____
_____

Message or Thoughts: ✉️
_____
_____
_____

Anniversary Guest List

Name :

Message or Thoughts:

_____

_____

Name

Message or Thoughts:

_____

_____

Name :

Message or Thoughts:

_____

_____

Name

Message or Thoughts:

_____

_____

Name :

Message or Thoughts:

_____

_____

Anniversary Guest List

Name : _____   Message or Thoughts: _____
_____   _____
_____   _____
                                       _____

Name _____   Message or Thoughts: _____
_____   _____
_____   _____
                                       _____

Name : _____   Message or Thoughts: _____
_____   _____
_____   _____
                                       _____

Name _____   Message or Thoughts: _____
_____   _____
_____   _____
                                       _____

Name : _____   Message or Thoughts: _____
_____   _____
_____   _____
                                       _____

Personnal Notes

NOTES

DATE: _____

NOTES

DATE:

NOTES

DATE: _____

NOTES

DATE:

NOTES

DATE: _____

NOTES

NOTES

DATE:

NOTES

NOTES

DATE:

NOTES

DATE:

NOTES

DATE:

NOTES

DATE:

NOTES

DATE:

NOTES

DATE:

NOTES

NOTES

DATE:

NOTES

DATE:

NOTES

DATE:

NOTES

DATE:

NOTES

DATE:

NOTES

DATE:

NOTES

DATE:

NOTES

NOTES

DATE:

NOTES

NOTES

DATE:

NOTES

DATE:

NOTES

DATE:

NOTES

DATE:

NOTES

DATE:

NOTES

NOTES

DATE:

NOTES

NOTES

NOTES

DATE:

NOTES

DATE:

NOTES

DATE:

NOTES

DATE:

NOTES

NOTES

NOTES

DATE:

NOTES

DATE:

NOTES

DATE:

NOTES

DATE:

NOTES

NOTES

DATE:

NOTES

NOTES

DATE:

NOTES

DATE:

NOTES

NOTES

DATE:

NOTES

DATE:

NOTES

DATE:

NOTES

DATE:

NOTES

DATE:

NOTES

DATE:

NOTES

DATE:

NOTES

DATE:

NOTES

DATE:

NOTES

NOTES

NOTES

NOTES

DATE:

NOTES

DATE:

NOTES

DATE:

NOTES

DATE:

NOTES

DATE:

NOTES

DATE:

NOTES

DATE:

NOTES

DATE:

NOTES

DATE:

NOTES

DATE:

NOTES

DATE:

NOTES

DATE:

NOTES

DATE:

NOTES

DATE:

NOTES

DATE:

NOTES

DATE:

NOTES

DATE:

NOTES

DATE:

NOTES

DATE:

NOTES

DATE:

NOTES

DATE:

NOTES

DATE:

NOTES

DATE:

NOTES

DATE:

Made in the USA
Las Vegas, NV
13 November 2024

11751930R00057